# SHTF Prepping:

*From Beginner to Badass. A SHTF Prepping Survival Guide for any Life-Threatening Situation or Disaster*

Zach Williams

The information in the following pages is broadly considered to be a truthful and accurate account of facts and as such any inattention, use or misuse of the information in question by the reader will render any resulting actions solely under their purview. There are no scenarios in which the publisher or the original author of this work can be in any fashion deemed liable for any hardship or damages that may befall them after undertaking information described herein.

Additionally, the information in the following pages is intended only for informational purposes and should thus be thought of as universal. As befitting its nature, it is presented without assurance regarding its prolonged validity or interim quality. Trademarks that are mentioned are done without written consent and can in no way be considered an endorsement from the trademark holder.

# Table of Contents

# Introduction

Congratulations on downloading *SHTF Prepping: From Beginner to Badass. A SHTF Prepping Survival Guide for any Life-Threatening Situation or Disaster* and thank you for doing so. The world is growing increasingly chaotic and downloading this book is the first step you can take towards actually doing something about it. The first step is also always the easiest, however, which is why the information you find in the following chapters is so important to take to heart as they are not concepts that can be put into action immediately. If you file them away for when they are really needed, however, then when the time comes to actually use them, you will be glad you did.

To that end, the following chapters will discuss the primary preparedness principles that you will need to consider if you ever hope to realistically be ready for a disaster of epic proportions. This means you will want to consider the quality of your shelter including the potential issues raised by its current location, how it can be best utilized in an emergency and various reinforcements or fortifications you may need to have on hand in case of an emergency.

With shelter out of the way, you will then learn everything you need to know about canning a wide variety of items including common fruits and vegetables along with less common items as well. Rounding out the three primary requirements for successful survival, you will then learn about crucial water storage principles and what they will mean for you. Finally, you will learn how building a root cellar is likely the best choice for storing all of your hard work.

There are plenty of books on this subject on the market, thanks again for choosing this one! Every effort was made to ensure it is full of as much useful information as possible, please enjoy!

# Chapter 1: Primary Preparedness Principles

It doesn't matter what metric that you are measuring, signs that there is trouble ahead can be found practically at every turn. Seeing the signs is one thing, preparing for them is another matter entirely as it is not something that can be done haphazardly at the last moment if you hope to be able to realistically provide for your family if the worst does, in fact, occur. When it comes to knowing that you are ready for what lies ahead, you need to ensure that you have a reliable supply of food and water, as well as a shelter that you can count on to help you weather the storm.

**Set your priorities**

There are plenty of options when it comes to ensuring that you have access to all three survival requirements when the time comes for you to need them, which means the first thing you are going to need to consider is what types of options are right for you. Survival options run the gamut from expensive and state of the art to cheap and homemade and the variety is enough to make many people throw in the towel before they even begin. The numerous options are manageable however, but only if you consider them one step at a time.

*Consider what you will need:* The very first thing you will need to determine is how well your shelter will survive as well as how much food and water you are going to realistically want to have on hand for when the worst happens. To figure out this amount you will want to keep in mind that you and your loved ones will be able to go as long as three weeks without any real food, three full days without any drinkable water and only three hours out in the elements in adverse conditions. Furthermore, it is realistic to assume that in major metropolitan areas the available stores of food on hand will run dry within less than a week without existing infrastructure to prop them up. With this in mind it is easy to reach the conclusion that you will need to have a minimum of six months of food and water on hand per person you plan on providing for in case of an emergency.

*Think about water:* While many families won't have the space or the means to store water that will last them for six months, a good starter goal is around two weeks' worth of water on hand for the family which means that each person will need 14 gallons, plus water for cooking and cleaning as well. What's more, that number should be upped by half a gallon each day during the summer months. If you're a family of four then this means that you will want to have around 70 gallons of clean, fresh water available at all times. While this might seem unmanageable on its face, the fact of the matter is that a 50-gallon water barrel is actually quite manageable and there are stackable five gallon options for smaller groups that will fit practically anywhere. A variety of water storage options are considered in chapter 4.

*Think about food:* At this point in the twentieth century, it was still exceedingly common for everyone, even those who lived in cities, to have a small plot of space set aside for a small garden if nothing else. Growing your own food and canning it for preservation was just a way of life and everyone routinely kept much more food on hand as a result. Fast forward to today and everything has changed, and hardly for the better; in fact, if you took away their ability to buy new food, most people would be unable to last a week with what is currently in their homes. In times of crisis this will have severe consequences as the grocery stores themselves are no better, keeping little more than a few days' worth of products on hand at a time.

When it comes to storing food, the first thing that you will want to do is ensure that the pantry space that you already have available is full of long lasting items that you will be able to count on for quite some time. While it will likely be quite expensive to purchase all of the required items in one fell swoop, the beauty of preparing for the future is that you have plenty of time to do so. Even if you only increase your food budget by $20 each week, you will still be able to have a stockpile of food available in less than six months, regardless of how many mouths you have to feed.

When taking the piecemeal approach, it is important to keep detailed notes relating to the dates of the items that you have purchased as well as when they are likely to have expired. While this might seem cumbersome at first, it will make it much easier to rotate foods out as needed, something you will want to take pains to stay on top of if you don't want to eventually find yourself back at square one unexpectedly.

While common foodstuffs are all well and good, if you are looking to plan for the long term, and don't fancy the idea of paying top dollar for high priced items packaged to outlast the sun, then investing in the traditional methods of food preservation is the most logical choice. While canning tools might not be cheap, they are going to cost much less in the long run, and the food you actually get to eat at the end of the day will be much healthier as well. Additional canning and preserving details can be found in chapter 3. A good mix of short term and long term food items is crucial to knowing that you are prepared for any scenario.

*Think about where you are going to keep it:* While planning out how much food and water you are going to be stockpiling, and how you are going to pay for it, it is equally important to ensure that you have the right space to store it all in. The best sort of storage spaces are those that are especially designed for food storage which means taking moisture levels, light levels and oxygen levels into account, even if you have already gone to all of the trouble of canning your food properly. When it comes to storing your food and water for maximum efficacy you are going to want to aim for a storage space that stays somewhere between 65 and 72 degrees F in temperature during the summer months for the best results. What's more, the space should be dark and dry to help keep things in their ideal state for as long as possible.

# Chapter 2: Preparing Your Home

When it comes to preparing to keep you and your family safe during an emergency, it is important to take food and water considerations into account if you hope to survive for any prolonged period of time completely off of the grid. These precautions will all be for naught, however, if you don't first take the time to ensure that your home is as ready as it possibly can be when it comes to withstanding a serious disaster as well as the resulting issues that are sure to come along with it.

*Take stock of your situation:* First things first, if you want to be prepared in case of an emergency, you are going to want to consider what your options would be like if a majority of modern infrastructure vanished overnight and you were actually confined to the slice of the world where you currently live. Consider what resources the area with 10 miles of your home has to offer and how quickly they would be depleted as well as the other types of concerns you would need to start dealing with immediately in order to ensure the long-term survival of your family or friends. It is important to consider all the major factors for your survival in your assessment as well as the likelihood of having to deal with individuals who may realistically be hostile; remember, forewarned is forearmed and you will always be more grateful that you prepared for a scenario, no matter how unlikely, than you would be that you overprepared for the reality of the matter at hand.

Once you have inventoried your local area, the next thing you will want to consider is your home itself. Consider its strengths and weaknesses both structurally as well as defensibly as you will need to consider booth if you plan on being prepared for anything. It is especially important to take measures to be ready to fortify windows and doors. The longer you plan on preparing for the inevitable the more advanced you can get with these types of preparations including high quality screens and security doors, though having the supplies on hand to board up weak points will certainly work as well.

At this stage, the type of preparations that you already have on hand aren't nearly as important as the fact that you have made it a point to take inventory of your current situation. The first step to serious preparation is getting started and it is the stumbling block for many individuals, simply because there is no deadline for completion. Don't let yourself get complacent, take stock of your home as soon as possible, once you have finished the process you will be glad you did. Finally, you will also want to have a general plan in place for where you will go in case something happens that renders your initial plan moot.

*Consider physical isolation:* It doesn't matter what the actual disaster is, one of the easiest things you can do to ensure the long-term survival of you and yours is isolate yourselves as much from the rest of the world as possible. Not only will this cut down on the risk of disease and infection, it dramatically reduces the risk of ancillary issues or violent incidents until a relative level of order has been restored. While you won't necessarily be able to isolate your family from the rest of the world completely (at least most people won't), a good rule of thumb is the less contact from the outside world the better.

To that end, it is important to understand what you can realistically do in order to create what is known as an island of physical isolation between your family and as much of the rest of the world as possible. While those who have acres of land to spare likely won't have to worry about this type of issue, the problem is magnified the greater the popular density in the area in which you live. As long as you have your own plot of land, however, then you can realistically prepare to limit your contact with other people during the most chaotic times of crises to the bare minimum.

Ideally you will want a secondary space outside of your home to take care of bodily functions if the utilities go, as well as to provide your family somewhere to go to avoid feeling trapped. The best option is a yard with sturdy walls on all four sides, though a secondary story deck would work in a pinch as well. Again, the specifics don't matter as much as the fact that you know what you need to do to fortify your space as much as possible at a moment's notice.

*Plan out how you will optimize space:* Preparing to defend your space is all well and good, but it just as important to have a firm grasp on how you will use the space if it suddenly becomes your entire world. You may need to consider additional sleeping and living arrangements for family members who do not always live in the home, which can make things difficult. You will also need to plan for where you will store all of the extra supplies that are required to truly be ready for anything. When making these types of preparations it is important to always have a plan in place for providing basic medical care as well as creating a quarantine zone in case the disaster is chemical in nature.

Studies show that when it comes to preparing for disaster situations the number one issue that most people run into unexpectedly is a lack of storage space, simply because it is so easy to underestimate the size of things that aren't there. As such, you will likely find more success if you find containers with specific measurements that fit into the existing storage space in your home which will allow you to know exactly how much space you have available at any given time. Furthermore, once you set aside space specifically for a survival prepping scenario, it is extremely important to resist the temptation to store something else in the empty space in the interim. If dedicated space simply becomes storage space then there will likely not be any of it left when the time comes, resist the urge and keep the space free of clutter.

*Clean your home as thoroughly as possible:* Starting today, it is important to keep your home as clean as possible, simply because you never know if or when you are going to lose access to fresh cleaning supplies. What this means is that you are going to need to go through every room of your home and remove unnecessary clutter, finish any organization projects you have been putting off and finally get around to fixing all the little things you always say you will find time to get around to later. Instead of continuing to put these types of things on the backburner, make an effort to take every aspect of prepping more seriously, including keeping your property ready for anything.

With all the little things out of the way, you will then want to give every surface a deep cleaning and then regularly clean with enough vigor to keep things at that state moving forward. While it is easy to nominalize this part of the process, the fact of the matter is that a cleaner environment is also a healthier and more organized and efficient one, three things that will benefit you regardless of the greater scenario that you currently find yourself dealing with. While the major changes are the ones that are talked about, sometimes the minor ones are going to be just as important.

*Be prepared to deal with cabin fever:* When it comes to preparing your home in case of an emergency, there is plenty of talk about what is needed to physically survive, but relatively little emphasis placed on mental health during times of extreme crisis and prolonged isolation. It is important to keep the mind sharp if you and your family hope to survive in the long term which is why it is as important to stockpile entertainment options of all types to ensure that you always have something to pass the time during the periods where it seems as though you may never be able to leave your home without worry ever again. While they have all declined in popularity over the past 20 years, cards, puzzles and good old fashioned books are all a great way to pass the time and keep your mind sharp so that you are ready for whatever is coming next. Furthermore, if you are religious, keeping a spare copy of your religious text of choice could very well be a literal life saver as well.

# Chapter 3: Preserving and Canning

When it comes to canning, the goal is to keep an item in a state of maximum freshness for the greatest period of time possible. This can be accomplished either through what is known as water bath canning or via a process called pressure canning. If you have never canned anything before then you will likely want to start with water bath canning as it requires less specialized equipment while still giving you access to numerous different types of food to can, including tomatoes, jams, pickles, jellies and more. If you are planning on going whole hog and canning an entire meal, including meat, then pressure canning will be the better choice.

It doesn't matter which path you choose to head down, when you start canning you will always want to ensure the food you choose to can is as fresh and all-natural as possible. Likewise, you will want to ensure that it is free of blemish or bruising as this will shorten the shelf-life of the end result, defeating the purpose in the process. The best-case scenario is to choose items that have been prepared within the previous 12 hours, though if you have just picked a piece of fruit or vegetable off of the vine then you will want to let it ripen at least 24 hours before canning.

Above all else, however, it is important to be extremely careful when it comes to performing the canning process as, when done incorrectly, canning can lead to severe poisoning or even death. These hazardous issues are much more likely to occur when an unapproved method of canning is attempted, specifically via steam canning, oven canning or microwave canning as these processes do not allow the jars to reach the temperature required for true canning to occur. Always be based on a recipe and if your results show any visible irregularities dispose of them at once.

*Prepare food for canning:* Before you will be able to can your goods for maximum freshness, you are going to need to be to able pack them into jars properly. The first type of packing is what is known as raw packing and it is done by simply placing the items to be canned into the jars moments before the jars are going to be sealed. This process is most appropriate for vegetables that are going to be canned using a pressurized system. The other type of packing is what is known as hot packing and it is useful for a wider variety of foods than raw packing. This method of packing is done by simmering food in boiling water prior to placing it into jars.

While it might not seem like much, it actually reduces the amount of air found in food, increasing its shelf life significantly. As an added bonus, the extra heat makes the seal the jar lid creates extra tight.

## Water bath canning

*Required tools*

- Ladle
- Spatula
- Tongs
- An implement for removing jar lids from boiling water
- Two large pots
- One funnel

When it comes to performing this type of canning process, it is important to never move forward without having a recipe handy to refer to if you need additional guidance. You will want to start by placing both pots of water onto the stove over a pair of burners set to a high/medium heat. Add the jars as well as the lids to the water and let them boil for a minimum of ten minutes. After the ten minute mark, you will want to remove the jar from the pot and fill it as per the recipe's instructions, taking special care to keep all air bubbles out of the jar.

Once you have finished filling the jar, ensure that the mouth is clean before placing the lid on the jar, followed by the ring and ensure the seal is as strong as possible. Once the lid is on tight, the next step is to return it to the first pot and place it in water that is a minimum of 212 degrees F for the amount of time as indicated in the recipe. Finally, you will want to ensure the vacuum seal on each jar has been achieved prior to storing.

*Tips for success*

- Never place more than 6 cups of fruit into a jar for preserves as more than this amount will prevent the fruit from setting properly.
- If you are unsure about the quality of your water, use 2 T white vinegar to sterilize it. Avoid vinegar that has an acidity of greater than 5 percent.
- To prevent illness, you should avoid moving your jars for 24 hours after you have finished the canning process. Additionally, at the end of that period, if the lids have not popped to signify a strong seal then you know that something is wrong. Never use a lid more than once.
- The amount of time that you will need in order to process your jars will vary based on the altitude where the process takes place. If you are at between 1,000 and 3,000 feet, then you can expect the process to take about 5 minutes longer than it otherwise might.

If you are above 3,000 feet but below 6,000 feet, then you can expect the process to take an extra 10 minutes and if you are above 6,000 feet then you can expect the process to take an extra 15 minutes.

## Pressure canning

While you will use many of the same tools and techniques with pressure canning as you would with water bath canning, the pressure canner itself ends up making all of the difference. While there are countless different pressure canners available on the market today, you will want to ensure that the one you choose is large enough to hold at least 4 single quart jars as anything smaller than that will likely not be powerful enough to handle the tasks that you will want it to tackle.

*Instructions:* First and foremost, you are going to want to fill the canner full enough to ensure that while going through the process you do not run out of water. You will not need the jars to be completely submerged in this process. They cannot be totally dry either. Additionally, don't worry about sterilizing the lids or the jars, clean jars and lids will work just fine. They will need to be hot for the best results, however, this can be accomplished by placing a few inches of boiling water into each after they have been cleaned.

With the jars prepared, you are going to want to fill them as per the instructions in the recipe before adding them to the rack inside the pressure cooker. With the jars secured, you are going to want to replace the cover on the pressure cooker and heat it to the point that it boils. Once it starts boiling you will want to vent the steam for the first 10 minutes before closing the vent and letting the internal pressure build to the desired level. The amount of time you will want to leave the jars in the pressurized state will vary based on the recipe you are using. After the desired period of time has elapsed you will want to let the pressure canner cool for 12 hours prior to removing the jars.

As with water bath canning, the amount of pressure that you will need to use will vary based on your altitude. With a pressure canner, however, you will need to also consider if you are using a canner that is a weight gauge or one that is a dial gauge. If you are using a pressure canner with a dial gauge, and you are canning at 2,000 feet or below, then you will want to set your dial at 11. If you are above 2,000 feet and below 4,000 feet, then you will want to set your dial at 12. If you are above 4,000 feet and below 6,000 feet, then you will want to set your dial at 13. If you are above 6,000 feet and below 8,000 feet, then you will want to set your dial at 14. If, on the other hand, you are using a pressure canner with a weighted gauge then you will want to use the 10 setting if you are under 1,000 feet and the 15 setting if you are above 1,000 feet.

## Fruit canning

When it comes to canning fruit, you can easily create your own canning syrup by combining sugar with water in a saucepan, adding a little heat and mixing well. If you want a light syrup, use two cups of sugar and one quart of water and if you want a thicker syrup use three cups sugar instead.

*Apples:* When it comes to canning apples, Granny Smith, Gala and Jona-Gold varieties tend to take to the process the most readily. Feel free to can apples using either canning method and keep in mind that 20 lbs. of apples will give you about 7.5 quarts canned. To properly prepare the apples, place them along with the syrup you have created into the second pot and let it boil. When it comes time to fill the jars, ensure that you leave about half an inch of space at the top of each, that each jar is free of air bubbles and that the mouth of each is clean. Finally, when it comes time to submerge the jars, do so for 20 minutes.

*Cherries:* It doesn't matter if you are canning sweet or sour cherries, the process is the same. It doesn't matter if they have pits or not, ten lbs. of cherries are likely to create four quarts of canned cherries. When it comes time to fill the jars, ensure that you leave about half an inch of space at the top of each, that each jar is free of air bubbles and that the mouth of each is clean. Finally, when it comes time to submerge the jars, do so for 25 minutes.

*Peaches:* You will find that roughly three pounds of peaches are needed to fill a quart jar. You will want to be sure that you boil the peaches for about 45 seconds, followed by an ice bath, prior to peeling to make the task much more manageable. Once they are peeled you will want to cover them in syrup immediately to prevent discoloration. Peaches remain just as delicious regardless if they are hot packed or raw packed, though if you choose to raw pack, be sure to fill as you go for the best results. On the other hand, if you are hot packing them you will want to cut the peaches directly into the syrup for the same results. When it comes time to fill the jars, ensure that you leave about half an inch of space at the top of each, that each jar is free of air bubbles and that the mouth of each is clean. Finally, when it comes time to submerge the jars, do so for 30 minutes.

*Apricots:* If you are planning to raw pack your apricots then you will not need to peel them, otherwise it is best that you do. Ten pounds of apricots will neatly fit into 9 pint jars. To prepare the apricots for the process you will want to slice them in half before placing them face down into the jars. When it comes time to fill the jars, ensure that you leave about half an inch of space at the top of each, that each jar is free of air bubbles and that the mouth of each is clean.

Finally, when it comes time to submerge the jars, do so for 25 minutes.

*Berries:* It doesn't matter what types of berries that you favor, the canning process is always going to be the same. You will always see better results when raw packing softer berries, though hard berries will be fine regardless. When it comes time to get down to it, you will find that 4 quart jars is enough for 15 lbs. of berries of all types. If you plan on hot packing your berries you will want to add in a quarter cup of sugar for each quart of berries before letting them sit for three hours prior to starting the process. When it comes time to fill the jars, ensure that you leave about half an inch of space at the top of each, that each jar is free of air bubbles and that the mouth of each is clean. Finally, when it comes time to submerge the jars, do so for 20 minutes.

## Vegetable canning

Vegetables of all types require a pressure canner in order to be stored effectively, you will need to add 1 tsp. canning salt to each jar as well.

*Tomatoes:* You will find that roughly ten tomatoes fit in each quart jar and that it doesn't matter if you remove the skin or leave them natural prior to canning. When it comes time to fill the jars, ensure that you leave about half an inch of space at the top of each, that each jar is free of air bubbles and that the mouth of each is clean. Finally, when it comes time to submerge the jars, do so for 25 minutes.

*Green beans:* You will find that 10 lbs. of green beans fit neatly into eight quart jars and that raw packing and hot packing are equally successful. To prepare the beans you will want to break each in half and clean them thoroughly. If you plan on hot packing them you will want to allow the beans to boil for five minutes and then drain them before packing them into the jars loosely and then adding fresh boiling water. If you are raw packing the beans then you will want to pack as many as possible into each jar. When it comes time to fill the jars, ensure that you leave about an inch of space at the top of each, that each jar is free of air bubbles and that the mouth of each is clean. Finally, when it comes time to submerge the jars, do so for 25 minutes.

*Corn:* When you can corn, you will find that it takes approximately 30 lbs. to fit into seven quart jars and that corn takes longer to can than other vegetables. In order to can corn successfully you will want to blanch it and then add it to cool water for the best results. You will want to hot pack the corn for the best results; do so you will want to pack it into the jar loosely before adding the boiling water on top. Prior to hot packing, you will want to let the kernels simmer for about 5 minutes. When it comes time to fill the jars, ensure that you leave about an inch of space at the top of each, that each jar is free of air bubbles and that the mouth of each is clean. Finally, when it comes time to submerge the jars, do so for 90 minutes.

*Carrots:* You will always want to peel your carrots prior to canning to reduce your risk of botulism as much as possible. Two and a half pounds of carrots are required to fill a quart jar. If you plan on hot packing the carrots, you will want to simmer the carrots for about five minutes before packing them into the jars lightly and covering them in boiling water. When it comes time to fill the jars, ensure that you leave about an inch of space at the top of each, that each jar is free of air bubbles and that the mouth of each is clean. Finally, when it comes time to submerge the jars, do so for 30 minutes.

*Potatoes:* As with carrots, you will always want to peel your potatoes prior to canning to reduce your risk of botulism. Ten pounds of potatoes are required to fill seven quart jars. If you plan on hot packing the potatoes, you will want to simmer the potatoes for about five minutes before packing them into the jars lightly and covering them in boiling water. When it comes time to fill the jars, ensure that you leave about an inch of space at the top of each, that each jar is free of air bubbles and that the mouth of each is clean. Finally, when it comes time to submerge the jars, do so for 30 minutes.

## Soup canning

Soup can only be canned effectively using the pressure canning method. When canning soup, you will want to avoid any additives such as noodles, milk, rice, flour or cream and to instead add those in after you have reheated the base. If you plan on including anything such as beans or peas, then you will want to cook them fully before canning them. When it comes to canning soup safely, ensure that all of the ingredients can be canned successfully individually for the best results.

## Meat canning

When it comes to canning meat, you are going to want to keep a few things in mind for the best results. First and foremost, you will want to remove as much gristle and fat as possible while also ensuring the integrity of the cut of meat is top notch. You can either hot pack the meat in accompanying broth or raw pack it normally. It is important to never attempt to can meat via a water bath and only ever used canned meat that has been created using a pressure canner. The time required to pressure can meat is much longer than the times required for vegetables, but all of that time is needed to ensure things work out properly. Be patient and the results will be worth it.

# Chapter 4: Storing Water

While storing food will certainly come in handy, it will all be for naught if you don't have enough water to keep everyone you care about alive long enough to enjoy it. Luckily, there are plenty of different options when it comes to storing water in the long term, many of which are outlined below.

*Find the right container:* First things first, you are going to want to choose the right type of container to use for your water storage needs as not all containers, even those that hold water perfectly well in the short term, are fit for doing the job in the long term. While not all plastics should be used for long term water storage, those with the label of 2, 1, 4 and 5 all can be reliably used to store water for a prolonged period of time.

If you are thinking about storing your water in a glass container, then you are going to want to reconsider for a number of reasons. First and foremost, it can break easily and is even subject to microscopic flaws which can then hold bacteria, even if the container is cleaned on a regular basis.

The only type of glass that can be used reliably is Pyrex, and even then, it is best to seek out alternatives instead whenever possible. All told, if you are looking to store a large amount of liquid for a prolonged period of time then stainless steel is going to be your best bet every single time. Stainless steel water containers are relatively common which means they can often be purchased quite cheaply and the water that stays within them can be considered safe for 40 years or more.

When it comes to storing your water safely in the long term it is important that you choose the right type of space for the best results. You are going to want to place it in a location that is structurally sound and unlikely to be in the path of the oncoming dangers you are hoping to prepare against. It should be someplace that is dry, cool and dark and the seal should remain unbroken until it is time to use the water to prevent contamination. Even then, if you have regular access to clean water then you will want to ensure that you swap out your reserves every six months to guarantee that things stay as clean and healthy as possible for when you really need it.

*Clean your water:* If you are storing a large amount of water for a prolonged period of time, then you are likely going to need to consider ways of keeping it clean if you need to replenish the source under less than ideal circumstances.

The first thing you will always want to include is chlorine. If you are drawing water from the tap, then it will already have enough chlorine in it to sanitize it completely; if that is not the case then you will want to add in two drops of chlorine for every two liters of water that you are storing. When it comes time to choose the right bleach for the job, it is crucial that you choose one that is no more than 5 percent chlorine. Once you chlorinate your water you are going to want to ensure that the container remains open for at least an hour prior to consumption.

If you are dealing with larger amounts of water, a good choice to consider is instead what is known commonly as pool shock. More officially known as calcium hypochlorite, a single pound of this additive will clean up to ten thousand gallons of water without issue. When you are purchasing calcium hypochlorite you will need to ensure that it is less than 78 percent pure, while still being more than 68 percent pure. Additionally, you will need to ensure that it is free of water softeners.

If you find yourself in a scenario where you are unsure as to the quality of the water that is available for you to drink, then a good choice is to consider using iodine in it before drinking. If you are unsure about water that otherwise appears to be clear, then you will only need to use 5 drops per gallon. If, however, the water is murky in addition to being suspect, then you will need to use at least 10 drops per gallon to achieve the desired results.

**Preparing for the long term**

While an ample supply of water will get you through a short to moderate period without access to new clean water sources, eventually those supplies are going to run dry. If you find yourself in a scenario where this is a very real possibility, then you may need to consider the options outlined below if you do not have ready access to a well on any existing property.

*Water filter:* If you have ready access to water, just none of it readily drinkable, then looking into a water filter is a reasonable choice. Water filters come in all shapes and sizes, which means that there is bound to be one that is perfect for your needs on the market somewhere no matter how big, or small, they are. You can also find purifiers that purify for various levels of impurities including things like bacteria, salt, even radiation using either fiber filters, other types of small filters or a type of ceramic. There are even UV filters that work with a connected solar panel to ensure you always have access to powered water filtration. If you are worried that you won't be able to drink existing water, there is a type of water filter to allay your fears. When considering various types of water filters you will want to ensure that the one you choose doesn't require replaceable filters as that rather defeats the purpose.

*Emergency still:* If you are in a location that has access to lots of non-potable water then what is known as an emergency still is a practical choice. This type of device works by collecting water before boiling it to remove all impurities and then collecting the resulting steam so that it eventually turns back into water that has been highly purified. These types of devices are often much larger and more complicated than a simple filter but they leave the water drinkable indefinitely and can be used to withdraw water from damp soil, urine, even plant matter. If you find yourself in need of a variation of this device in a hurry, a sheet made of a thick plastic strung over the grouping of liquid and a hot day will provide much the same type of effect.

*Water pump:* If you are going to need to eventually draw water from an underground source then that means that you are going to need a water pump of some type. The most common water pumps are hand-operated and can then be rigged to run on everything from wind to animal power. If you are planning on using a hand pump, then you will need to determine just how deep you will have to go before you hit water. If your water table is below 40 feet, then you will need a deep pump instead of one that is rated as shallow.

**Digging a well**

If you don't have a well, but you do have a decent sized piece of property then there is a good chance that you have the capacity to create a well of your very own in many parts of the world. Digging your own well is not quick or easy but it can be extremely rewarding if you take the time to do it properly. Consider the following before you get started to ensure that your journey to dig a well isn't over before it even begins.

*Know the area:* While this might seem obvious, it is surprising how little many land owners know about their property. First and foremost, you need to be aware of any leach field or septic tanks that can be found on the property as bacteria from these types of areas can be found as much as 100 feet underground. Additionally, you will want to avoid all types of rocky outcroppings as they are generally a good indicator of additional rock underground that can make the process of digging infinitely more difficult and can cause the resulting water to have a strong mineral taste as well.

With the major hazards out of the way, you will then need to look into the details of the area and find out where the best place to begin actually is. If you're in the United States, the best place to start when it comes to finding details in your particular area is the US Geological Survey which can be accessed at Water.USGS.gov. With the specifics, out of the way, the next thing you will need to determine is what the local laws are like regarding the permits you will need to dig your own well if you are interested in keeping everything above board.

*Digging a well:* A hand dug well can be as simple or as complicated as you choose to make it. However, there are a few things that you will always want to keep in mind if you hope to have the easiest time of it possible. First and foremost, this means that you will want to line the top of your well also known as casing; this simply means surrounding the outer edge of the well with stones to prevent excessive contamination of the well. As an added bonus this will keep the opening of the well stable and help save your hard work from a cave-in. You will know that you are finished digging your hand dug well as soon as the bottom of your hole starts to fill with water.

# Chapter 5: Long-term Storage Basics

While modern refrigeration technology is so prevalent in many parts of the world that it doesn't warrant thinking about, the fact of the matter is that there are plenty of storage options out there that don't require the grid in any way shape or form. If you are looking for a way to store your freshly created canned goods then the best way to do so, with or without electricity, is always going to be a root cellar.

Root cellars have remained a reliable food storage alternative over the centuries for their ability to keep food up to 40 degrees cooler than the outside temperature while also ensuring that it does not freeze in the winter. They will never be as uniform as more modern food storage methods, however, and can experience as much as a 10-degree variance between the top of the cellar and the bottom. In addition to temperature, root cellars naturally magnify the amount of humidity in the air, keeping fresh produce at a higher state of freshness for a prolonged period of time. The natural humidity of most underground spaces means that everywhere outside of extremely arid climates should naturally be well suited to the task.

**Planning for your root cellar**

*Consider your humidity level:* When it comes to building a root cellar, the first thing that you will need to consider is the type of items that you will be storing. You will always want to aim for a low temperature, however, if you are storing primarily canned goods you will want an overall lower level of humidity than if you are storing a greater amount of fresh produce. If your humidity gets too high, then your metal lids might rust which is why you should make it a point to invest in a hygrometer to ensure you always know your current humidity level to an exact percentage. If you find that you have a level of humidity that is consistently higher than you might like, then you will want to include concrete floors in your cellar as well as a barrel of rock salt to help soak up the moisture in the air or increasing the overall level of ventilation

*Consider your physical location:* The part of the world that you live in will frequently play a large part in the type of storage method that will be the most effective in your root cellar. If you live in a part of the world with very mild winters, then you will be unable to store many fresh vegetables or fruits at proper temperatures. You will, however, be able to easily store dried fruit as well as nuts and grains. If you live in a colder climate, then you will instead be afraid of things freezing completely which is why you will need to consider steps like improved insulation as well as air vents that are warmed by the sun to bring in extra warm air on cold winter days. In a pinch, you can even use hanging old-fashioned light bulbs as well as barrels of water to keep your food from freezing solid.

*Consider the legal requirements:* Determining the legal requirements for building a root cellar in your area might be tricky, simply because of how far root cellars have fallen out of fashion in the modern world. Unfortunately, just because you might not be able to find the right form online, doesn't mean no permit is required which means you will likely need to visit a government building to get the proper paperwork. If you get lucky, you will find that the area you live in considers a root cellar to be a form of shed that is exempt from building permits. Adding a root cellar to an existing basement can often be considered renovating an existing space which may not require a permit in some areas, but still will in others so it is best to always know what your local requirements are before getting started.

## Getting started

Even if you don't know exactly what form your root cellar is going to take, you likely know what you hope to one day keep in it. This is, in fact, the only thing you need to know at this phase, so if you know what you want to store then you are actually ahead of the game. It is important to always start with these details as certain combinations of produce simply cannot be stored together for a prolonged period of time with any real success due to natural processes that take place when they sit for a prolonged period of time.

For example, plums, pears, peaches and many vegetables including both tomatoes and cabbage are known to produce ethylene gas which means they will ensure any potatoes or carrots that you store near them without the proper ventilation will always be exceedingly bitter. Knowing this, you would then want to store these types of produce near the top of your root cellar and also loosely cover them with soil to keep excretions to a minimum. You will want to give the same treatment to onions and Chinese cabbage as well as their unique flavors will leech into nearby neighbors if you aren't careful.

Besides produce, you will want to consider the other types of things that you will want to house in your root cellar. The cool, dark space is a natural fit for beer, wine and cider as well as curing meats including ham and bacon along with smoked meats in the winter if you know your root cellar stays under 40 degrees F for more than a month at a time. If it reaches that temperature, then you will also be able to store milk for several days along with grains and nuts as long as the humidity is not too high and precautions are taken to ward off insects. If you are just getting started then a good base of produce to include would be apples and potatoes which will keep for the greatest period of time, this is followed by kohlrabi, onions, squash, cabbage, turnips, beans, pumpkins, nuts and peppers which have been dried.

*Bare minimum requirements:* If you are looking to stash some food as quickly as possible, the easiest way to do so is to start with a traditional metal garbage can that has been completely buried as it will at least give you a stash spot should the need arise. If you take this route all you need to do is dig a hole that is a little larger than the overall diameter of the can and deep enough into the ground that it will sit comfortably some four inches beneath the top soil when things start to freeze up for the winter.

After you have placed the can in the ground you can then insulate it even more using straw to fill the remaining space. After you have placed the lid on the can you will want to coat it in sturdy plastic to prevent anything from getting in as well as additional straw, or even mulch, to help what is inside retain a reliable temperature. You will find the best results with this type of storage by keeping root vegetables in the trash can. Doing so will allow you to keep potatoes and the like fresh all winter long.

*Choose a design for your root cellar:* While the most popular design for a root cellar is likely that which is built into the side of a small hill, many modern root cellars simply head straight down instead, often with a door, or pair of doors between the cellar and the outside world. If you have access to them, many types of metal storage containers that have been buried in the ground make a great starting point for root cellars of all sizes.

Regardless of the style that you choose to pursue, what makes the root cellar so effective is the fact that the soil that surrounds it provides such a reliable means of insulation, keeping it both warm and cool in equal measure. To achieve this effect, however, you are going to need at least three or four feet of soil on all sides otherwise you are going to be missing out on the full effect. If you have the ability, you should actually try for a full 10 feet of coverage on all sides, especially if you have weather that trends heavily in one direction or another.

When it comes to honing in on the right design for you, it is important to consider any restrictions that put constraints on the cellar based on the property that you are placing it in, on or under. The most popular root cellar designs these days include a pair of rooms that are separate from one another to ensure that the humidity stays much higher in one room than it is in the other. This will provide you with the ability to readily store items of numerous different types without having to worry about potential issues down the line. These setups typically place the room which has a lower level of humidity outside of the room with the higher level of humidity for the best results.

When making these types of decisions you will definitely want to keep the overall space of the end result in mind as otherwise it can quickly get out of hand. If you are planning to feed a family of four, then you will want to plan for two 8x8 rooms as a minimum. If you are hoping to prepare to feed more than four people you will want to add in an extra two square feet of space for each additional individual that you plan to feed.

*Choosing the right location:* When it comes time to finding the right location for your root cellar, it is important to take special care to consider the parts of it that will ultimately be directly exposed to the outside world. You will want to take special care to ensure that any part that does never receives direct sunlight as this can easily skew the final temperature and negate your hard work in the process. To ensure that you are getting the right angle on the sun you will want to always build on the northern facing side of any hill or in a space that is otherwise naturally in the shade 100 percent of the time. Additionally, you will want to take special care to ensure that the roof will not see any leaks or other types of runoff from rain or other elements. To ensure that these hazards are not insurmountable, take care to look into doors that are slooped or other types of easy draining options.

If you plan on building a root cellar in an existing basement, there are several things you will want to keep in mind for maximum ease of use. First and foremost, if you place it in the northeastern corner then you will be able to use the foundation for two sides of your cellar. Additionally, you will want to ensure that you use plenty of insulation as your home will naturally put off much more heat than the surrounding environment. What's more, you will also need to include a ventilation system that is expressly for use with the root cellar to avoid any issues.

If your plan is to build a root cellar that heads directly into the ground, the first thing that you will need to do is ensure that the desired area is free of roots before you start. Not only will having to dig through roots make the process much more time consuming than it would otherwise be, it will also lead to a structure that is less stable overall. Next, you will need to be aware of how the space you are preparing is going to drain. If the soil you are digging through is naturally sandy then you likely won't have many problems, otherwise you will need to construct your cellar at a sloping angle to improve drainage. Additionally, if it regularly reaches 25 degrees F or lower where you live in the winter months then you will need to ensure your cellar is completely below the frost line and that it is insulated with more than just dirt to keep your produce from freezing completely.

*Don't neglect air flow:* It is important to ensure that your root cellar has reliable air flow which means you will want to plan out where you want the air vents to go before you actually start construction. Having the right amount of air flow will also ensure that odors or, even worse, ethylene gas, will be able to freely leave the space as needed while also helping keep the temperature either warmer or colder depending on the time of year. You will need to have at least a pair of vents, one at the top of the space and another at the bottom, to circulate air properly, though multiple sets are always going to be preferable.

Regardless of how you plan out your space, it is important that you ultimately choose to go with vents that include a filter with which to keep out any contaminants that might ruin all of your hard work. These vents will also need to have the ability to be closed against the elements should the need arise. The eventual vents that you choose to use will need to be capable of turning to catch or prevent local winds as needed.

To ensure that all of your eventual shelving gets the right amount of air flow, you are going to want to make it a point of spacing the shelves at least an inch apart from one another as well as any walls. Each of the shelves should also leave an inch of space between the tops of items and the next shelf and be open backed as well. These precautions will allow the air to move around each of the items unimpeded on all sides. This means that you will not want to store anything directly on the ground for the best results, small stands or racks are always going to be preferable.

*Pest control:* If you are worried about common burrowing pests making their way into your root cellar, the first thing you will want to do is line the walls, floor and ceiling of your space with a fine wire mesh that won't allow much of anything to squeeze through. If you have more serious pests in your area, then you will want to plan accordingly to ensure that things like poison are kept far away from the produce to prevent cross contamination. To prevent pests from hitching a ride in on the produce that you are storing it is important to check everything that you are going to bring into the space thoroughly beforehand. What's more, you will need to check all of the items again once or twice a week for the first two months to ensure that everything remains as it first appears.

# Chapter 6: Root Cellar Variations

While several different types of root cellars are going to be discussed in this chapter, it is important to keep in mind that none of them use any wood in their construction unless it has already been waterproofed using a food-safe solution. This is an extremely important step if you plan on using wood as otherwise you can easily loose an entire year's worth of storage due to mold and odors.

*Above the ground basement root cellar:* When it comes to creating a root cellar in your basement, you are going to want to start in the area which is already the most humid. If you can find a place that has at least 80 percent humidity, then you know you are well on your way to success. Someplace near a sump pump is often a great choice. If you are planning on building in a corner to take advantage of existing walls then it is important that you think about the movement of the sun throughout the day to ensure you aren't accidentally choosing an area that receives a lot of heat, even if you are building indoors.

To ensure your air flow is at the level you want it to be for this type of build, you will want to acquire at least one pair of 3-in. PVC piping. These pipes should be long enough that they make it all the way through the wall at the top as well as at the bottom. It is important to prevent this ventilation from running through the property at all, if possible, to prevent temperature changes in the home from negatively affecting the cellar. After you have placed the pipes where you want them to go, you will want to cap the vents by adding on a blast valve and securing it properly to provide you with full control over the airflow into and out of your space.

With airflow firmly established, the next thing you will want to do is find the right walls for the cellar which in this case means something that is inherently rot resistant such as cedar or another wood that has been treated to prevent water damage. An easy way to go about this is to use a pair of cedar 2x4s attached to the ceiling and floor respectively with a panel of what is known as green board, the substance shower stalls are often made from, in between. Once you have the outside panel in place, the next thing you will want to do is to add in fiberglass insulation both inside and out, remember your goal is to create a space that has as much of a limited air flow as possible.

With the walls built, the next thing that you will need to do is find the right shelves for the job. The best choice in most cases is going to perforated metal shelving as it is naturally resistant to the elements and will prevent water from pooling around your produce. When it comes to choosing the right door, or pair of doors, to protect your root cellar you can purchase something that is prefabricated or craft one yourself using .25-inch plywood hung on a pair of studs. You may also find it useful to select a door that can be opened in halves to make it easier to reach things close to the door without letting all of the cold air that has settled to the bottom of the space out and forcing the process to start all over again.

*Root cellar built with earth bags:* If you are considering building into a hill or directly into the ground then a root cellar constructed of earth bags is a natural choice. All of that dirt has to go somewhere anyway and there is no better place than directly into the construction of the cellar. Earth bags come in a number of varieties and they are simply construction grade bags designed to easily be filled with dirt. To successfully create this type of root cellar you are going to need the aforementioned earth bags, a cedar or other type of treated door frame, PVC piping, barbed wire, gravel and balling twine.

One of the most cumbersome parts of the entire process is actually filling the earth bags, though it goes much more quickly with a pair of individuals working through it. In this arrangement, one person will need to be exclusively in charge of removing any vegetation from the dirt as well as large rocks and filling the bags while the second person then takes them into position.

To get started, you will want to begin by digging out the space you will use for a room that is eight square feet. Once this has been completed you will then need to add in any drainage that you plan on using, 4-inch PVC piping will do the trick as long as it has been filled with holes to help maximize drainage. With the piping in place you will want to cover it will 12 inches of gravel that has been thoroughly tamped down. Once this has been finished you will have the floor of your root cellar properly in place.

The end result of this type of process will naturally be a circle, with the construction process consisting of layering earth bags on top of one another in increasingly smaller circles. As such, if you hope for the space to come together as planned you will need to precisely measure how big the diameter of the first layer is going to need to be to ensure you reach the ceiling in the predetermined period of time. Additionally, you will need to consider any space you need for a doorway as well as ventilation at the start to ensure things come together properly.

You will want to fill the early bags with a mixture that is about 20 percent concrete to give them a little bit of extra weight, though after the first three or four layers you can switch exclusively to dirt. After you finish a layer you will want to tamp it down thoroughly and then lay two lines of barbed wire across it to ensure everything stays where it is meant to be. You will find that each layer will naturally be smaller than the last, though this is not a process that you should rush to ensure maximum stability.

After you have completed the structure you will want to wrap the entire thing in at least two layers of heavy polyethylene plastic before insulating it using dirt, or something more insulating as needed. To prevent against unwanted moisture, you will then want to liberally coat the inside of the space in a plaster that is lime based to allow the space the ability to breathe while still protecting against undue moisture. It is important to find the right shelves for the job to ensure they do not take up undue space as many standard shelving units will be cumbersome in a round space.

*Prefabricated root cellar:* If you like the idea of burying something in the ground but don't want to purchase a prefabricated root cellar directly, the most cost effective option is often going to be a septic tank that has never before been used. Tanks which have flaws that render them otherwise unusable in a traditional sense can often be retrofitted for root cellar purposes for pennies on the dollar, though you will need a tank that is at least 2,500 gallons to provide you with the room you will need to move around relatively easily. A tank of that size, that is otherwise unusable, will likely cost around $800. When you go to purchase a tank, it is important to always ask the seller to remove the included partition to save yourself some work.

After you have purchased a new septic tank and found the place that you are planning to put it, be sure to put down a thick layer of crushed stone rather than simply placing it into the dirt, as this will make it easier to ensure the tank is level before you get started. After you have the tank in place you will then need to cut holes for the ventilation as well as the door for which you will need a saw capable of cutting through concrete. To get started you will want to mark a spot on the tank roughly four inches from the bottom on the opposite side from that which already has a hole. This spot will mark the bottom edge of your door.

When it comes to cutting the holes for your ventilation and door it is important to always take appropriate precautions when using a concrete saw, additionally, you may need a sledgehammer to complete this project properly. When it comes to finding the right door, your best bet is going to be finding an insulated steel door premade and already hung in a frame which you can just bolt into place. As such, it is important to know what door you will be using before you cut your door hole.

When it comes to properly cutting your vent holes you will want to ensure they are always a minimum of 4 inches wide, there should already be a hole about that size on one end which means in most cases you will only need to cut a single additional hole. To make cleaning out your root cellar extremely easy, you will also want to include a hole in the center of the bottom portion that can be used as a drain.

With all of your holes created, all you need to do is put it all together. This includes sealing the original access hatch that typically sits at the top of the tank. You will then want to cover this access point in several layers of thick plastic to ensure it remains waterproof for years to come. Once this has been completed all that is left is to fill in the space around the root cellar with either dirt or a more insulating material as needed. Additionally, you will want to create a retaining wall near the primary doorway to prevent dirt from getting inside the cellar.

# Chapter 7: Surviving A Natural Disaster

Natural disasters can be life threatening both during the event and for several days afterwards. Aside from preparing for them beforehand, there are things that you must do in the midst of the crisis and afterwards to ensure the survival of yourself and the others around you.

*Earthquakes:* Earthquakes are caused when underground faults are broken and the pressure buildup is released in the form of seismic waves which cause the ground to shake. Buildings and houses are very dangerous places to be in during an earthquake. At the first sign of an earthquake, the safest place to be is out in the open with no structures around you; this is because during an earthquake the building or house could collapse while you are still inside of it and can lead to serious injury or death.

If you find yourself trapped in a building or house while an earthquake is happening and the exit is blocked or too far away, then the first step you should take is to take cover under something sturdy. Your best bet is to either look for the closest bathroom, doorframe, or anything else that is likely to offer protection in the event of damage to the foundation of the building.

Once the earthquake has stopped it is still dangerous to be in the building or house, because it may have loosened up the foundation and the entire thing could collapse at any moment. The first thing you need to do is help secure everyone out of the building or home as fast as possible and to leave unimportant things behind because you can always go back for them later. After everyone is safe outside you need to wait there for a couple hours because another earthquake could occur and the secondary round of damage is likely to be much more intense than the first.

*Hurricanes:* Hurricanes are caused when rising warm moist air displaces cold air high above the atmosphere. Hurricanes are extremely dangerous and luckily today we have the technology to track them and find out where they are likely to occur. By keeping up to date with the news and paying attention to warnings in the weather you should be able to prepare for one early enough to protect you, your family, and your belongings. Strong buildings and basements are excellent places to hide while a hurricane is passing by as they offer a lot of protection.

Weak houses and buildings should be evacuated weeks or days prior to the arrival of the hurricane, because hurricanes can have wind speeds of over 100 miles per hour which can easily rip a ceiling right off of an old home. If you are unprepared and a hurricane does arrive, never go outside unless you are moving to a safer location. Standing outside is very dangerous because during a hurricane, debris is flying around everywhere and you can easily be hit with something that can cause serious injury. Even if you don't believe your home will hold up to a hurricane it is still better to be inside of it then outside however while inside of it you need to find a spot that you believe offers the most protection. Find anything strong and sturdy that you can take cover under that can withstand parts of the ceiling falling on top of. It should also be really heavy or attached to the floor so that the hurricane does not pick it up.

During a hurricane, many stores, hotels, apartment complexes, schools, and other buildings will allow people to take shelter until the hurricane passes by. These places offer free food and water and will also broadcast the news so that you know when it is safe to return to your homes.

*Floods and Tsunamis:* The result of multiple powerful waves crashing onto the shore of a beach, tsunamis will destroy and carry almost everything in its path. Inside of a tsunami will be a lot of very harmful debris that the tsunami picked up from houses, trees, cars, and other things that are on the ground.

Shorelines and the areas next to beaches are extremely dangerous places to be during a tsunami as they are most vulnerable to destruction. The best possible way of ensuring safety is to get to higher ground. Buildings and houses have a risk of being destroyed however some houses if they are strong enough will stay put but the inside of the house will be flooded. The worst case scenario would be if a tsunami is arriving and you do not have enough time to move to higher ground; if such event happens, then you want to get a ladder and have everybody climb up to the roof of the house and stay put.

*Avalanche:* When snow on a mountain that was perfectly balanced becomes disturbed, thousands of pounds of compact snow comes rushing down the mountain. An avalanche can be extremely scary because you will usually see and hear it coming but will not have enough time to run away from it. If you ever plan on going out in the snow always go with friends and always bring a GPS tracking device with you. After an avalanche, it is likely that you will be trapped under compact snow and not have much room to move or breathe, which can eventually lead to death from suffocation as the snow takes the consistency of almost cement.

To maximize your chance of survival you want to always be strapped with someone else so either they can find you or you can find them, and before the avalanche does hit you want to make a pocket of air by covering your head. Then take a deep breath of air and brace for impact. If possible, try grabbing onto a nearby tree or boulder. During the passing of the avalanche, if you happen to be swept away try your best to swim upwards to stay as close to the top of the snow as possible. Before you get buried, stick one hand in the air so that you can have a sense of direction where the surface is. People stuck in snow might be disoriented and not know which way they should be digging so you can try spitting and see which way gravity pulls your saliva. Also, try your best to dig out a breathing area in front of your face, this should supply you with at least 30 minutes for rescuers to come and get you. If you know that you are buried deep, then try your best to conserve your breath because it is almost impossible to dig through the snow with your bare hands. If you happen to have a snow shovel, then you can give that a try as well. Being patient and waiting for help is the only thing you can do in some situations.

*Tornado:* Tornadoes almost never appear without a warning and are classified either from F-0 to F-5. F-0 being only a mild tornado and F-5 being the most destructive. Tornadoes can get powerful enough to lift up cars and wipe out houses so they should always be taken seriously and preparation should always be done before a tornado is expected to arrive.

You should always stay clear of the path of a tornado as much as possible, and you definitively have to take immediate action and drive to a safer location ahead of time. If at home and a tornado is likely coming your way, then you need to find a safe spot in your house. Look for areas in the center of the house and in small rooms. Also, stay away from the outsides walls of the house and from windows because there is a chance that the tornado can throw debris right through them. Basements are also safe places to take shelter in case of a tornado because the entire house is a shield for that one area.

When outside during a tornado try to get as low to the ground as possible and if you can, then get inside of a ditch and take cover there. If inside of a vehicle, always get out of it because a tornado can easily tip it over or pick it up and throw it in another direction. However, if you are far enough away from the tornado you should also attempt to drive away from its path; if you are on a road that allows you to go over 60 miles per hour, you can most likely outrun the tornado.

# Chapter 8: First Aid Techniques

When you find yourself facing an emergency that is going to require first aid, the first thing you will want to remember is that remaining calm in any situation, no matter how severe, is the most important thing to do. By remaining calm you are preventing yourself from doing anything foolish that will worsen the situation. You also have the time to think out the best course of action you need to take. If you ever find yourself in a emergency just understand that the problem is only as bad as you think it is and you are not the only one to have ever been in that situation.

*Cuts and broken bones:* Cuts, bites, and scratches from wild animals should always be cleaned out with clean water first or preferably a disinfectant, then you want to stop the bleeding with whatever you have available at the time (strips of cloth work great for this purpose). Every few hours you should change the bandages. Fractures and broken bones can be a little more serious, as the victim is usually unable to move on their own. To treat a fracture until help arrives you need to move the injured to a safe location and stop any bleeding by creating a tourniquet followed by a splint.

If you are dealing with a person who is bleeding excessively, then ideally you are going to want to use sterile gauze to apply pressure directly to the wound. Only when this is unavailable do you want to use what is known as homemade dressing, aka anything that is not gauze, since you can actually make the situation worse by adding elements that can lead to infection into the wound. Still, if you are in the middle of nowhere a shirt that might not be the cleanest is certainly better than bleeding to death. If a steady supply of pressure is not enough to stop the bleeding completely, the next thing that you will want to do is use a tourniquet.

*Create a tourniquet:* While the use of a tourniquet has critics on both sides of the issue, the truth of the matter is that as long as the tourniquet is applied properly and not left on unnecessarily, then it can easily save a person's life with little to no negative side effects. While concerns of nerve damage and limb loss are not unfounded, recent studies show that less than half of one percent of all people who are treated for blood loss via the use of a tourniquet require limb amputation because of the tourniquet and less than two percent of all people experience any type of nerve damage. Damage from prolonged tourniquet use doesn't begin for upwards of two hours, and upwards of eight hours of continuous use are required before amputation becomes a realistic option.

While a professionally made tourniquet is nice to have, it is hardly a practical addition to your daily carry, especially as there are so many other things can be used for the same purpose in a pinch. The belt at your waist, a long sleeve shirt, shoe laces, bicycle tubing, the strap from your backpack or even a bra are all ready-made for tourniquet duty should the need arise. Along with an object to act as a makeshift tourniquet, you are also going to need something to keep it tight, officially known as a torsion device. What you are looking for here is anything that is long and thin; if you are in the wilderness then there are likely to be plenty of sticks in the area that will work just fine.

When it comes to applying a tourniquet, it is important to only use it on limbs and never the neck; this may seem self-explanatory, but people tend not to think clearly during a crisis. For starters, you are going to want to wrap the tourniquet around the affected limb about two inches towards your core from where the wound occurred, taking special care to avoid joints or major arteries. When in doubt, move closer to your core as opposed to further away.

With the positioning completed you will then want to tie the tourniquet in place using a single knot tied overhand; you will then want to set the torsion device directly on top of the knot before tying it in place with either a square know or another knot tied overhand.

*Create a splint:* If you find that you need to create a splint to deal with an injured party member, the first thing that you will need to do is find something that is rigid enough to ensure the fractured area remains stabilized. Something made of wood is the most common approach, though even a rolled newspaper will work in a pinch. When it comes to securing the splint to the afflicted area you are going to want to consult the list of items that can be uses as a tourniquet because they can all pull double duty as splint fasteners as well.

Don't forget to attend to any bleeding prior to dealing with anything in need of a split. Likewise, never move an injured individual without applying a splint as this will almost always cause the injury to become more severe. With that in mind, you are going to want to set the split so that it reaches far enough above the afflicted area to align with the nearest joint on either side. As such, if you needed to splint your forearm, you would want the splint to reach from your wrist to your elbow. When you tie the splint on, you will want to ensure that it is tight enough to prevent undue movement and loose enough to prevent a loss of blood flow. Finally, once the splint has been properly secured it is important to check it regularly to ensure that it is not cutting off blood flow, as the area might already be numb and a change might not be noticed otherwise.

If you need to put one of your hand, or someone else's, into a splint then the first thing that you will want to do is to ball up something soft and place it in the palm of the hand that has been injured to give it a bit of structure for the remainder of the split. Once the fingers of the hand are closed around the object, the next thing you are going to want to do is wrap the entirety of the hand in a large cloth, leaving just the finger tips exposed. This cloth should move in a horizontal direction across the hand starting at the thumb and moving towards the pinky. With this done, you will then want to ensure the hand is bound properly using additional ties, taking care to not make things so tight that they cut off circulation.

*Burns:* To treat a burn, you have to identify the cause of the burn and act accordingly. Burns from the cold temperature should be warmed by placing the area of the burn in warm water or by blowing warm air on the burn. Burns from hot liquid should be cooled by running cold water over it for 10-20 minutes and never use ice. If someone is burned from being electrocuted, then you should separate them from the current and immediately check for a pulse and apply CPR if necessary. With the torsion device in place, you will then want to rotate it so the tourniquet tightens against the limb just until the point where bleeding stops, it is important to not put more constraints on the limb than necessary, so stop the moment the blood loss subsides. Finally, you will want to ensure the torsion device is going to remain in place by taking the ends of the second knot and tying it to the limb and the tourniquet respectively.

*Choking:* Choking is a fatal accident that can happen anytime you are eating. First aid for choking starts off with giving five back thrusts which is basically using the palm of your hand and hitting in between the person's shoulder blades. After that is done you want to perform five abdominal thrusts (also known as the Heimlich maneuver). To do the Heimlich maneuver you need to stand behind the person and give them a bear hug with your hands on their belly button and pull in an upwards angle. This process should be repeated until the person can breathe regularly.

*CPR:* Cardiopulmonary Resuscitation should be performed immediately if someone has little nor no pulse and is unresponsive. This could be a result of drowning, electrocution, poisoning, or fainting. The first step is to call for medical help immediately and then begin CPR. By performing CPR you are allowing oxygenated blood to flow around the body of the victim. Without this oxygenated blood, the brain is not receiving any oxygen and in only a matter of minutes the victim's brain will start to receive serious damage. It only takes eight minutes without blood flow for the brain to die.

After help is on the way to you, the next thing to do is to position the person in need of CPR on their back with their head facing the sky and tilt their head at an angle to ensure that their airway is unrestricted. You will then want to put your hands on their sternum and, with your arms straight, push onto the person's sternum 30 times in a quick manner. This step is called the chest compressions and the amount of strength used should vary depending on who is receiving CPR chest compressions should be administered at a rate of 100 pumps per minute. For young children and old people, you should use little force as their ribs may break. When performing chest compressions your patient's ribs may break during the process, so as soon as you start hearing the cracking you want to immediately stop the compressions for a few seconds and then resume the process.

After performing 30 chest compressions, the next step is to breathe for the person. First, you want to make sure that their chin is up and head tilted back to clear all airways into the victim's lungs. Next, pinch the nostrils and make an airtight seal with your lips onto your patient's and breathe into them. You should also keep an eye over the chest of the victim and see if it is rising up and down as you breathe into them. You need to apply two breaths and immediately start doing chest compressions again. This should be repeated over and over until help arrives or the victim starts responding and is breathing on their own.

*Poison and venom:* If you feel that you or someone else has ingested or otherwise come into contact with a poisonous plant, then immediate action is required as time is of the essence. The first thing to do is to recognize the symptoms. Someone who is poisoned may be confused or behave in an erratic fashion, they may have difficulty breathing, exhibit signs of vomiting, or have a redness or overall discoloration around their face and hands. If you are not in a position to get traditional medical attention, the first thing that you will want to do is to induce vomiting. After that, you need to rinse out the mouth of the victim with water. If poisoned on the skin, then you need to get soap and water and rinse it out for 15 – 20 minutes. If poison gets in the eye, then you need to rinse out that area for 20 minutes.

If you were bit or stung by an insect or spider, then you need to get away from the nesting places of those insects and remove any stingers that are still in the skin. Clean the area out with soap and water and then apply an ice pack onto the area to reduce swelling. If bit on the arm or leg you should keep that area as close to the ground as possible to reduce the amount of venom that spreads.

Some species of snakes can be completely harmless where other species are extremely venomous. Snakes to look out for are the rattlesnake, cottonmouth, and copperhead. If bit by any snake check for symptoms of venom which include swelling, nausea, dizziness, fainting, weakness, convulsions, vomiting, diarrhea, rapid pulse, and loss of muscle coordination. If available, you should also add an antibiotic to the wound. It is also important if you can either take a picture of the snake or if you can safely kill it and bring it with you. This is so that if a medical team arrives you can show them what kind of snake it was and they will quickly know exactly which antivenom to use as all snakes have different types of venom. If no other option is available, you will want to quickly make a small incision above the area that was bitten and then suck on the wound in an effort to draw out the snake's venom.

In the United States, all poisonous snakes, save for the coral snake are what are known as pit vipers. As such, if you see a fat snake with a big head and slit pupils with what are known as heat pits on the end of their nose, then you know it is poisonous. As a general rule of thumb, if you come across a snake that is quite thin then you do not need to worry about it being poisonous. The coral snake is an exception to just about every rule regarding poisonous snakes, which means that you want to remember that if the pattern is red and black, it's safe Jack; meanwhile, if its red and yellow then it could kill you fellow.

# Conclusion

Thanks for making it through to the end of *SHTF Prepping: From Beginner to Badass*. Let's hope it was informative enough and able to provide you with all of the tools you need to achieve your goals whatever it is that they may be. There is still much more to lean on the topic of survival and expanding your horizons is the only way to find the mastery you seek.

The next step is to stop reading and to take action by doing whatever it is that you need to do in order to ensure that you and those you care about will be properly taken care of should the need arise. If you find that you still need help getting started, you will likely have better results by creating a schedule that you hope to follow including strict deadlines for various parts of the tasks as well as the overall completion of your preparations.

Studies show that complex tasks that are broken down into individual pieces, including individual deadlines, have a much greater chance of being completed when compared to something that has a general need of being completed but no real time table for doing so. Even if it seems silly, go ahead and set your own deadlines for completion, complete with indicators of success and failure. After you have successfully completed all of your required preparations you will be glad you did.

Once you have finished your initial preparations it is important to understand that they are just that, only part of a larger plan of preparation. You best chances for overall success will come by taking the time to learn as many vital skills as possible. Only by using your prepared status as a springboard to greater preparation will you be able to truly rest soundly knowing that you are prepared for anything and everything that life decides to throw at you.

Finally, if you found this book useful in anyway, a review on Amazon is always appreciated!

www.ingramcontent.com/pod-product-compliance
Lightning Source LLC
Chambersburg PA
CBHW060204290526
45789CB00003B/1155